Lillian C. Poole Elementary
1002 Wayside Lane
Dallas, GA 30132

Paw Prints

French Bulldogs

by Kristine Spanier

Bullfrog Books

Ideas for Parents and Teachers

Bullfrog Books let children practice reading informational text at the earliest reading levels. Repetition, familiar words, and photo labels support early readers.

Before Reading

- Discuss the cover photo. What does it tell them?
- Look at the picture glossary together. Read and discuss the words.

Read the Book

- "Walk" through the book and look at the photos. Let the child ask questions. Point out the photo labels.
- Read the book to the child, or have him or her read independently.

After Reading

- Prompt the child to think more. Ask: Have you ever seen a French bulldog? Would you like to play with one?

Bullfrog Books are published by Jump!
5357 Penn Avenue South
Minneapolis, MN 55419
www.jumplibrary.com

Library of Congress Cataloging-in-Publication Data

Names: Spanier, Kristine, author.
Title: French bulldogs / Kristine Spanier.
Description: Minneapolis, MN : Jump!, Inc., 2018.
Series: Paw prints | Includes index.
Audience: Ages 5 to 8. | Audience: Grades K to 3.
Identifiers: LCCN 2017039655 (print)
LCCN 2017044184 (ebook)
ISBN 9781624967719 (ebook)
ISBN 9781624967702 (hardcover : alk. paper)
Subjects: LCSH: French bulldog—Juvenile literature.
Classification: LCC SF429.F8 (ebook)
LCC SF429.F8 S63 2018 (print) | DDC 636.72—dc23
LC record available at https://lccn.loc.gov/2017039655

Editor: Jenna Trnka
Book Designer: Molly Ballanger

Photo Credits: cynoclub/Shutterstock, cover; Pixtural/Shutterstock, 1; Eric Isselee/Shutterstock, 3, 9, 22; anetapics/Shutterstock, 4; ardea.com/ Jean-Michel Labat/Pantheon/SuperStock, 5; Dobre Cristian Leonard/Shutterstock, 6, 23br; paul prescott/Shutterstock, 6–7; Aaron Amat/Shutterstock, 8, 23tr; Patryk Kosmider/ Shutterstock, 10–11, 16–17; NatalieShuttleworth/ Getty, 12, 23bl; Csanad Kiss/Shutterstock, 13 (left); Goldschmidt Photography/Shutterstock, 13 (right), 23tl; Magdalena Bujak/Alamy, 14–15; Anna Goroshnikova/Shutterstock, 18–19; CREATISTA/ Shutterstock, 20–21; Nejron Photo/Shutterstock, 24.

Printed in the United States of America at Corporate Graphics in North Mankato, Minnesota.

This book is for Phil Larsen.

Table of Contents

A Frenchie for a Friend

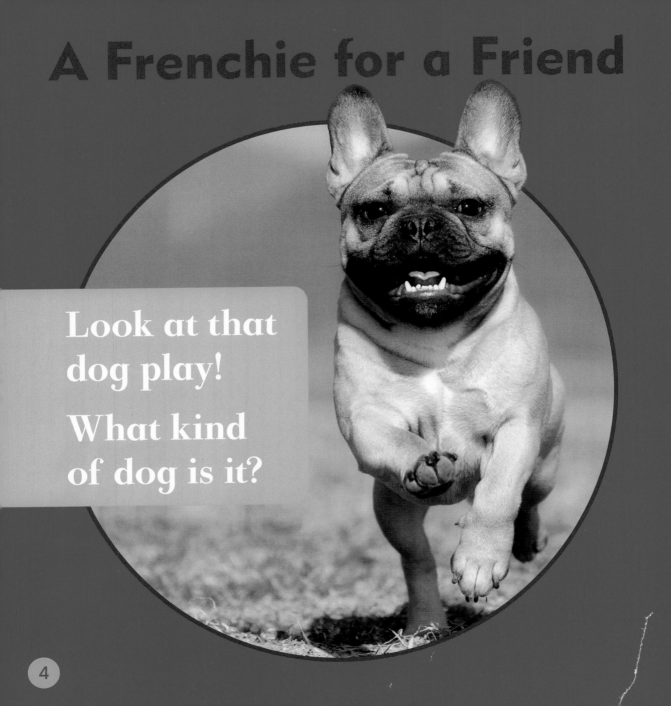

Look at that dog play!

What kind of dog is it?

It is a French bulldog!

They used to live
only in France.

Now they live
all over.

We call them
Frenchies.

France

fold

They have short snouts.
They have folds.

8

Their bodies
are small.

But they
are strong.

9

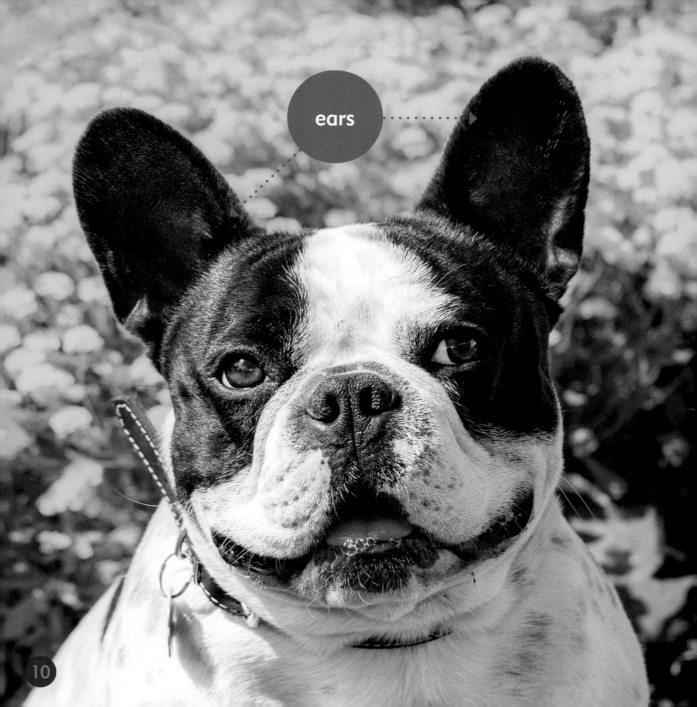

ears

Frenchies have
ears that stand up.

The ears are big
for a small dog.

The coat is short.
Pet one.
It feels smooth.

Frenchies come in many colors.

Which ones?

White, gray, and brindle.

brindle

They are alert.

Why?

To protect their families.

Frenchies sleep a lot, too.

Do they love to play?
Yes!

Frenchies love to
be with people.

Do you want to play
with a Frenchie?

A French Bulldog Up Close

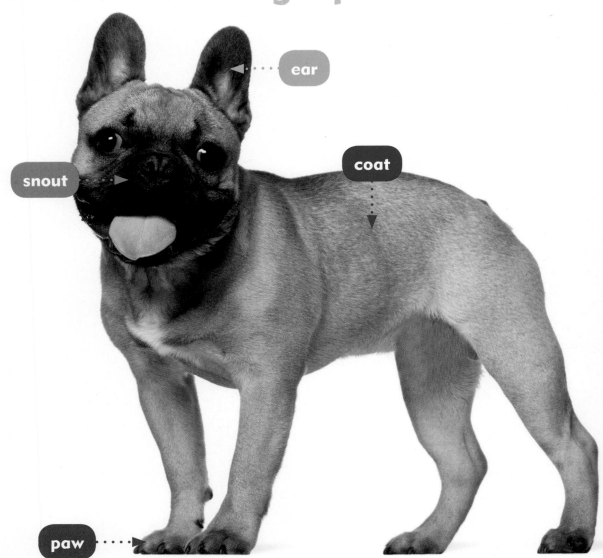

ear

snout

coat

paw

Picture Glossary

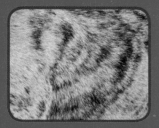

brindle
A dog's fur patterned with specks and streaks of light and dark markings.

folds
Lines or wrinkles in skin.

coat
A dog's fur.

snouts
The noses and mouths of animals.

Index

To Learn More

Learning more is as easy as 1, 2, 3.

1) Go to www.factsurfer.com

2) Enter "frenchbulldogs" into the search box.

3) Click the "Surf" button to see a list of websites.

With factsurfer.com, finding more information is just a click away.